Sayings of
Chairman Kim

If you wish to receive our lists of forthcoming titles, please send your request to the following address :
Robert Davies Publishing,
P.O.Box 702, Outremont, QC, Canada H2V 4N6

Sayings of Chairman Kim

Avril Phaedra Campbell
in her own words

ROBERT DAVIES PUBLISHING
MONTREAL – TORONTO

DISTRIBUTED IN CANADA BY

Stewart House,
481 University Avenue, Suite 900
Toronto, Ontario M5G 2E9

☎ (Ontario & Québec) 1-800-268-5707
(rest of Canada) 1-800-268-5742
Fax 416-940-3642

Copyright © 1993 Robert Davies Publishing,
a division of l'Étincelle éditeur Inc.

ISBN 1-895854-011-3

Table of Contents

ON NATIONAL DEFENSE AND PEACE

Lizzie Borden took an axe
and gave her mother forty whacks;
When she saw what she had done
She gave her father forty-one.

(Anon.)

Sayings of Chairman Kim

The removal of the nuclear threat has in many ways made the world less safe. There are all sorts of ways in which the new world configuration can create problems.

Toronto Star, March 27, 1993

It is highly premature to beat our swords into ploughshares.

Globe and Mail, January 5, 1993

The challenge we face now as members of the international community is to define the rules and principles by which we will join with other countries in trying to stop aggression and trying to prevent the development of a world where no country feels safe on its own, where all countries feel they have to arm themselves to the teeth because the international community can not act to protect them.

House of Commons, February 16, 1993

ON THE PUBLIC PURSE (Variations on a theme)

There's a sucker born every minute.
Phineas T. Barnum

Sayings of Chairman Kim

Most Canadian know that when you want to get finances in order, you confide them to a woman.

Leadership debate,
April 22, 1993, Montreal.

We cannot be a caring society if our purse is empty.

House of Commons, December 12, 1988

All the arguments that suggest that the national debt is somehow a figment of the government's imagination... are spurious.

House of Commons, May 9, 1990

Hand in hand with fiscal responsibility comes social responsibility.

House of Commons, May 9, 1990

JUSTIFYING THE GOVERNMENT'S INACTION ON CHILD CARE :

There is not a country in the world which meets its child care objectives.

House of Commons, May 9, 1990

Without addressing the problem of public debt, the government of Canada cannot address the question of income disparity in Canadian society.

House of Commons, May 9, 1989

Sayings of Chairman Kim

The sad reality of debt is that it feeds on itself…it places the nation on a treadmill.

House of Commons, May 9, 1989

JUSTIFYING THE EH-101 MILITARY HELICOPTER PURCHASE :

Are we talking numbers here or are we talking philosophy?

House of Commons, February 25, 1993

As a participant in the process of developing expenditure restraint guidelines, I asked questions about this project, but I was extremely satisfied with the justification given to this project.

Globe and Mail, February 26, 1993

Sayings of Chairman Kim

I am convinced the helicopter decision was the correct one... Canadians have to understand it costs money to do these things.

Victoria Times-Colonist, January 19, 1993

and yet...

Public spending has gotten out of control at all levels. Everything becomes entrenched. We almost never cut or evaluate. It is an agonizing, deep philosophical question we have to go through — but we should go back to square one and evaluate how we deliver those services.

Sayings of Chairman Kim

Vancouver School Board, November 1981

There is no limit to the good you can do, but there is a limit to the good you can afford.

House of Commons, February 28, 1992

**ON LACK OF PROGRAM FUNDING
TO HELP GET PROSTITUTES
OFF THE STREET :**

The reality of budgetary constraints, the multitude of issues competing for government's attention and the need of the government to spend money where it's more needed...It is open to question whether such projects would have much impact on prostitutes given the reality of the minimum wage that is available after having completed most training programs.

House of Commons, March 20,1991,

quoted by Sheila Copps

ON NATIVES

Fasten your seatbelts.
It's going to be a bumpy night.
Bette Davis, in *All About Eve*

Sayings of Chairman Kim

The right to self-government is part of every Canadian's birth right, and aboriginal Canadians are no exception.

House of Commons, April 24, 1989

Let us not insult Aboriginal Canadians by portraying them as passive wards of the State.

House of Commons, April 24, 1989

ON THE OKA CRISIS
I categorically refuse to equate the confrontation in OKA to pure and simple civil disobedience. Weapons are not the tools of

civil disobedience. Violence, effective or threatened, profits nobody.

House of Commons, September 25, 1990

If a Chinese youth gang in Vancouver appeared on the scene with masks and AK-47s, would they have been treated with that kind of patience?

House of Commons, September 25, 1990

Anyone who knows the native people of Canada knows that they are not sitting back waiting for government to save them.

House of Commons, April 24, 1989

ON THE CONSTITUTION

"My idea of an agreeable person, "
said Hugo Bohum,
"is a person who agrees with me".
Benjamin Disraeli

Sayings of Chairman Kim

The constitution has to reflect the reality of the country, or it will not work.

House of Commons, March 27, 1990

Quebec constitutes a distinct society within a country where all provinces are equal.

House of Commons, March 27, 1990

ON NATIONAL UNITY

Cheer up, the worst is yet to come.

Philander Chase Johnson

Sayings of Chairman Kim

The greatest threat to our national survival is the perception in the regions of Canada that the cost of Confederation is too high.

House of Commons, December 12, 1988

ON JUSTICE

Either he's dead or my watch has stopped.
Groucho Marx, in *A Day at the Races*

Sayings of Chairman Kim

I am not sure that the ease with which people violate the law is necessarily a reason not to have particular laws.

House of Commons, May 4, 1990

I think I have changed the way the Department of Justice operates.

Globe and Mail, December 12, 1992

ON SOME JEWISH GROUPS PRESSING FOR ACTION ON WAR CRIMINALS:

There are certain groups who, if they were happy, they'd have nothing to say to the press.

Toronto Star, August 13, 1992

Sayings of Chairman Kim

All of us want a bill that will preserve the safety of the Canadian public and at the same time improve the administration of the gun control system.

House of Commons, December 6, 1991

ON POVERTY

Indocilis pauperiem pati.

Horace

Sayings of Chairman Kim

There is nothing quaint about poverty.

House of Commons, December 12, 1988

ON THE
EXPERIENCE
OF WOMEN

It is a capital mistake
to theorize before one has data.
Sherlock Holmes
(Sir Arthur Conan Doyle)

Sayings of Chairman Kim

For millions of years women have catered to the male ego, only to produce a breed of male with utter delusions of grandeur. Women have a moral duty to save the world from the terrible mess men have made of it.

Ubyssey, November 1965

I would describe myself as a feminist, but aren't all forms of sexual segregation discriminatory?

Vancouver School Board, April 1982

There are women's groups in this country that don't like me very much. I don't really mind... We don't all think alike, we are not ideological clones of one another, we don't march in lockstep. My goal has been, not to define one simple view of the world as it relates to women, but to open the door to women.

Declaration of Candidacy, 1993

ON FEMINIST SOLIDARITY

Approving another Conservative Member's calling Sheila Copps a slut :

The Member from Hamilton East is the source of some of the more outrageous statements. I think you have to see these things kind of as a provocation.

Ottawa Citizen, September 19, 1991

Sayings of Chairman Kim

ON HOMOSEXUALITY

It's the only type of sexual aggression men have ever experienced and to be hit on, to be propositioned in that way, is deeply offensive. My reaction is, "welcome to the world of women".

Toronto Star, December 1991

ON A WOMAN WHO WAS MURDERED BY HER HUSBAND WITH A CROSS-BOW

One has to try to be sensible, not to be knee-jerk every time some device is used for killing.

Ottawa Citizen, November 19, 1991

ON THE CANADIAN IDENTITY

What is the answer?
In that case, what is the question?
Gertrude Stein, upon her deathbed

Sayings of Chairman Kim

We have been exposed over the years to an ever increasing volume of feature films, televised programs, music and books from the United States. In spite of that, our feeling of Canadian identity has not been reduced. Quite the contrary. It is even stronger today.

House of Commons, December 12, 1988

Sayings of Chairman Kim

In Canada, we have learned to balance the onslaught of American culture with our own reality. It is that ability to balance which is one of the chief characteristics of Canadians, which is why, perhaps, a Canadian has been defined as someone who can make love in a canoe.

House of Commons, December 18, 1988

Sayings of Chairman Kim

Political scientists identify two distinct political cultures in Canada, one being Quebec and one being British Columbia....We will not take our place fully in Confederation until the federal civil service is full of bilingual British Columbians.

British Columbia Legislature,
June 26, 1987

ON THE PARLIAMENTARY EXPERIENCE (IN THE HEAT OF DEBATE)

No one provokes me with impunity.
Motto of the Crown of Scotland

Don't do damage to your jaws over there, or your knees.

House of Commons, June 18, 1990

REFERRING TO IAN WADDELL :

The honourable Member is a lawyer and a lawyer of some skill... I have great respect for the honourable Member. He is, in fact a fine and distinguished member of the British Columbia Bar and has practised with some distinction. Notwithstanding that my father occasionally used to whip his butt in the courtroom, he is highly regarded by the Campbell lawyers... Whip his writ!

House of Commons, September 25, 1990

Sayings of Chairman Kim

I hope he does not do too much damage to his tendons with all that knee-jerking. I suspect there will be a good deal more.

House of Commons, April 24, 1989,
referring to Mr. Skelly

I'm glad the trustee said he was speaking emotionally because he wasn't speaking intelligently. Put a can in it, Rankin.

Vancouver School Board, 1982

One of the problems of rising in the House to speak toward the end of a speaking list is that it is very tempting to spend one's time allocation correcting the errors that have been made in the speeches of the Members of the Opposition.

> *British Columbia Legislature,*
> *April 1987*

I do not have anything to learn from the honourable Member

> *House of Commons, March 20, 1991*

REFERRING TO A QUESTION FORM NDP MEMBER RUSSEL MACLELLAN :

Regrettably, volume does not improve the coherence of the honourable Member's comments.

> *House of Commons, March 20, 1991*

Sayings of Chairman Kim

The kindest interpretation that can be put on the honourable Member's question is that it reflects the complete ignorance of the structure of complex commercial transactions.

House of Commons, March 5, 1991,
referring to a question
from David Kilgour, Liberal

The honourable Member's question is not only insulting, but it is false and misleading.

House of Commons, March 5, 1991

Sayings of Chairman Kim

If I am playing politics, I am a real piker in that department, I assure you.

House of Commons, March 10, 1993

Oh, forgive me. I haven't stood up for a day or two;…and I must be losing my touch by not picking up on the irony of the honourable Member for Victoria.

British Columbia Legislature,
December 4, 1987

[This bill] is very complex because clearly [the Opposition] don't understand it. I suspect some of them haven't read it; I suspect after three pages their lips get tired.

British Columbia Legislature,
April 14, 1987

I'm sorry, honourable Member. Are words of two syllables a little difficult for you to understand? I hope those scabs on your knuckles aren't distressing you too much.

British Columbia Legislature,
March 17, 1988

Sayings of Chairman Kim

I do have an IQ in the three digits, and I'm prepared to stand up in this House and discuss these things.

British Columbia Legislature,
December 4, 1987

ON ABORTION, AIDS, HEALTH AND MORALITY

In the real dark night of the soul
it is always three o'clock in the morning.
F. Scott Fitzgerald, in *The Crack-Up*

Sayings of Chairman Kim

PARAPHRASING THE OPENING LINE OF TOLSTOY'S ANNA KARENINA :

All welcome pregnancies are in a sense alike; but each unwanted pregnancy is unwanted in its own way. The existence of an unwanted pregnancy is a circumstance unique to the woman involved.

House of Commons, November 21, 1989

I do not accept the notion that a foetus has the same rights as a born human being.

House of Commons, November 21, 1989

Sayings of Chairman Kim

I am among those Canadians who are very comfortable without a law on abortion because from my perspective I feared a law which would attempt to generalize about what is basically an experience that cannot be generalized...But I can say quite sincerely and with a clear heart that this bill(C-43) is actually better than no law.

House of Commons, November 21, 1989

Sayings of Chairman Kim

It is a great pity that there is an over-fixation on AIDS, which is perhaps one of the least concerns in our society right now with respect to infectious disease...

British Columbia Legislature,
November 25, 1987

I don't think that religious views or even family upbringing are sufficient in this day and age to deal with what is a very provocative and sexually loaded culture.

British Columbia Legislature,
April 3, 1987

ON RUNNING
AND SERVING

I will not accept if nominated,
and will not serve if elected.
*General Sherman, on being urged
to stand as Republican candidate
in the U.S. election of 1884.*

It is a silly game where nobody wins.
Thomas Fuller

Sayings of Chairman Kim

I decided to enter federal politics when I heard John Turner misrepresent free trade at a speech in Whistler. I couldn't believe what I was hearing. It curled my hair. This wasn't the old, bumbling John Turner.

Interview with The Toronto Star,
November 1988

ON WHY SHE RAN FOR OFFICE

It's important that quality candidates stand for election.

Vancouver Magazine, April 1988

Sayings of Chairman Kim

ON THE SOCREDS, A FEW WEEKS BEFORE SHE RAN FOR THEM :

I am not a part of this government and I don't feel any obligation to defend it.

Vancouver Sun, July 16, 1983

AND AFTER HER ELECTION :

I am reminded of Paganini, who used to give concerts where he would break three strings on his violin in order to show his virtuosity on one string. I hope that my lack of preparedness will inspire me, like Paganini, to heights of address.

Maiden speech, British Columbia Legislature, March 16, 1987

Sayings of Chairman Kim

By the end of this campaign, you will know very much more about my views on the economy than you ever knew about those of Pierre Elliott Trudeau, even after he was Prime Minister for 16 years.

Leadership declaration speech, 1993

ON HER CHANCES OF GETTING INTO THE FEDERAL CABINET

I would be surprised if I wasn't in consideration.

Victoria Times-Colonist,
December 16, 1988

Sayings of Chairman Kim

ON WHY SHE DIDN'T GET INTO THE BC CABINET

For some reason the premier didn't want to put me in the cabinet. A lot of my colleagues wanted to see me there.

Victoria Times-Colonist,
December 16, 1988

O N   H E R S E L F

My candle burns at both ends;
It will not last the night;
But ah, my foes, and oh, my friends—
It gives a lovely light!
Edna St. Vincent Millay,
in A Few Figs from Thistles

Sayings of Chairman Kim

As an intellectually-oriented person, I like to socialize with people who read the same things I do and have a similar level of education, but I genuinely like ordinary people. I think it's very important to realize that a lot of people that you're out there working for are people who may sit in their undershirt and watch the game on Saturday, beer in hand...I suppose these people would find me as boring as I would find them.

Vancouver Sun, July 3, 1986

Sayings of Chairman Kim

I have discovered I don't need to be loved by the public.

Vancouver Magazine, April 1988

I was afraid that I would be seen as the candidate who has substance without charisma.

Leadership Declaration Speech

The comparison between me and Madonna is the comparison between a strapless evening gown and a gownless evening strap.

Vancouver Sun, November 4, 1992

Sayings of Chairman Kim

Seriously, the notion that the bare shoulders of a 43 year-old woman are a source of prurient comment or titillation, I mean, I suppose I should be complimented.

Vancouver Sun, November 4, 1992

I'm a sucker for highly intelligent men.

Vancouver Sun, July 3, 1986

ON LAWYERS

The first thing we do,
let's kill all the lawyers.
William Shakespeare, Henry VI

Sayings of Chairman Kim

Once you start releasing the text[of the Charlottetown accord], you will put it in the hands of the lawyers who will argue about what it means.

Montreal Gazette, October 2, 1992

I wonder if I might address this because the honourable Minister is not a lawyer and I am.

British Columbia Legislature,
November 26, 1987

ON TRADE UNIONS

The Social Contract is nothing more
or less than a vast conspiracy of human
beings to lie to and humbug themselves
and one another for the general Good.
Lies are the mortar that bind
the savage individual man
into the social masonry.

*H.G. Well*s

There is a widespread public disenchantment with organized labour... I believe the credibility of labour organizations depends upon apparent justice and fairness in their operations, and that includes a willingness to recognize the needs of the market economic system. These are needs that are recognized much more clearly by the American union organizations, but for some reason or other there is hostility in Canada and I think some of it derives from the origins of some of our union leaders.

British Columbia Legislature,
April 16, 1987

Unions are unfair and...they require greater legislation.

British Columbia Legislature,
April 16, 1987

Whatever ill will the public may think of politicians, it appears that they think even worse of labour unions.

British Columbia Legislature,
April 1987

Sayings of Chairman Kim

I believe the credibility of labour organizations depends upon a willingness to explore new forms of relationships between labour and management. I believe that if we are to move into a progressive economy in the 21st century, we must be willing to look beyond the traditional adversarial relationship.

British Columbia Legislature,
April 1987

Sayings of Chairman Kim

I am reminded by the opposition of another provision in Orwell, and I am thinking in particular of *Animal Farm,* where the animals are exhorted to chant the ideological position : four legs, good; two legs, bad. What I hear from the New Democratic Party opposition is a very similar kind of chant, and that is : unions good, management, bad.

British Columbia Legislature,
April 14, 1987

Sayings of Chairman Kim

I'm seeing the unacceptable face of trade unionism.

Vancouver School board, September 1982

I hope [the teachers] get kicked in the ass.

Vancouver Province, October 30, 1983

ON THE FREE TRADE AGREEMENT

Well, Mr. Baldwin!
this is a pretty kettle of fish!
Queen Mary, during the abdication crisis

Sayings of Chairman Kim

How can Canada continue to be a caring society and invest in its future human capital without a vibrant and diversified economy capable of paying the bill?

House of Commons, December 12, 1988

The Free Trade Act democratizes the Canadian economy by giving to the regions what central Canadian industries have long enjoyed, access to a significant regional market...The Free Trade Agreement does more for regional development in Canada than any policy in our history.

House of Commons, December 12, 1988

Sayings of Chairman Kim

Make no mistake, protectionism has distorted our economy to the detriment of all Canadians.

House of Commons, December 12, 1988

Both the manufacturing and the service sectors have realized that the path to greater prosperity lies in removing the training wheels of protectionism.

House of Commons, December 12, 1988

Sayings of Chairman Kim

**ON OPPONENTS TO THE
FREE TRADE AGREEMENT :**

Ignorance is bliss, I guess. But it's frustrating when you know things about it and you see the stupidities. I have to pick and choose which ridiculous statement I answer, and that is frustrating.

*Victoria Times-Colonist,
November 19, 1988*

What are you people so afraid of?

*To hecklers at Vancouver Centre,
March 27, 1993 (Toronto Star)*

ON THE
ROLE OF
THE STATE
AND ON
DEMOCRACY

Every country
has the government it deserves.
Joseph de Maistre, 1811

Sayings of Chairman Kim

As a philosophical Conservative, I have a great distaste for dealing with human problems in the abstract. I am often reminded of the statement of Edmund Burke, perhaps one of the great founders of philosophical conservatism, in his commentary on the French Revolution written in 1790, that the French Revolutionaries saw men as abstractions and in seeing them as abstractions, they forgot that they were human. It has been one of the guiding principles of my life to try never to lose sight of the human dimension of an issue.

House of Commons, November 21, 1989

Our government sees the role of government in Canadian society to strengthen individuals, to strengthen people in these communities, to give them the wherewithal to stand on their own two feet.

House of Commons, May 9, 1989

I believe that government has a right to legislate according to its own philosophy.

British Columbia Legislature,
March 5, 1987

Sayings of Chairman Kim

Governments are elected to govern, not batten down the hatches.

British Columbia Legislature,
April 28, 1987

I do not want to reinvent wheels that are already rolling happily along.

House of Commons, May 7, 1992,
quoted by J. Chretien,
re problems of infrastructure,
crime and social issues in Canadian cities

Sayings of Chairman Kim

Democracy is not just a question of putting a piece of paper in a ballot box every four years. It means something more than that. To be totally enfranchised, you must know that your reality will be considered in the making of public policy.

PC Leadership declaration speech

Democracy is not something a small number of people do *to* everybody else; it is not even something they do *for* everybody else. It should be something they do *with* everybody else.

PC Leadership declaration speech

Sayings of Chairman Kim

The challenge faced by democratic societies is to recognize that our values are often in conflict with each other.

House of Commons, September 25, 1990

ON LEADERS
(in general)

From each according his abilities,
to each according to his needs.

Karl Marx

Sayings of Chairman Kim

A great political leader is not someone who has all the answers. A great leader is someone who understands the questions and can lead the process of finding solutions.

*Leadership speech
to Socred convention, July 1986*

and in particular...

Every hero becomes a bore at last.

Ralph Waldo Emerson

Sayings of Chairman Kim

(REFERRING TO BRIAN MULRONEY):

He is an extraordinary leader, an extraordinarily intelligent person with a great passion for this country and he inspires great loyalty...Every time I go somewhere with the Prime Minister I see warmth, I see great respect...We're all very excited the Prime Minister has made it clear that he'll lead us into the next election and everybody is just feeling very good.

Montreal Gazette, October 30, 1992

ON A FELLOW TORY (PARAPHRASING GILBERT AND SULLIVAN'S <u>IOLANTHE</u> :

He did nothing in particular...I think that could characterize Bill Davis' approach to government.

British Columbia Legislature,
April 28, 1987

REFERRING TO ED BROADBENT :

His comments in this House today reflect not only a considerable amount of intellectual dishonesty, but a great deal of ignorance...I think it is not intellectually sound.

House of Commons, May 9, 1990

Sayings of Chairman Kim

REFERRING TO BILL VANDER ZALM :

I only wish I knew him before his lobotomy.

March 1988
(Quoted in Toronto Star, March 27, 1993)